eXplore

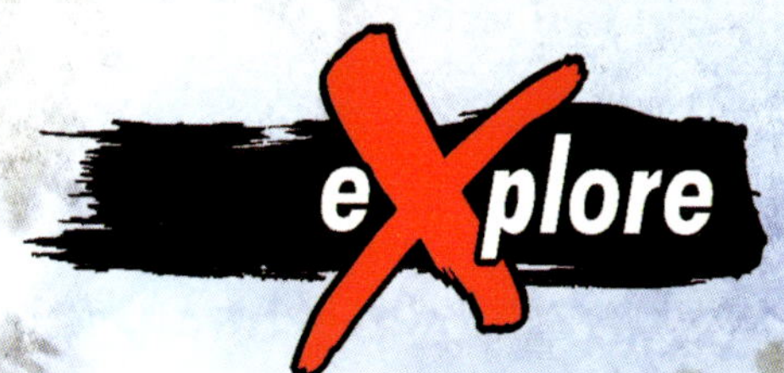

MY WILD FARM

Working with Nature

R.T. Watts

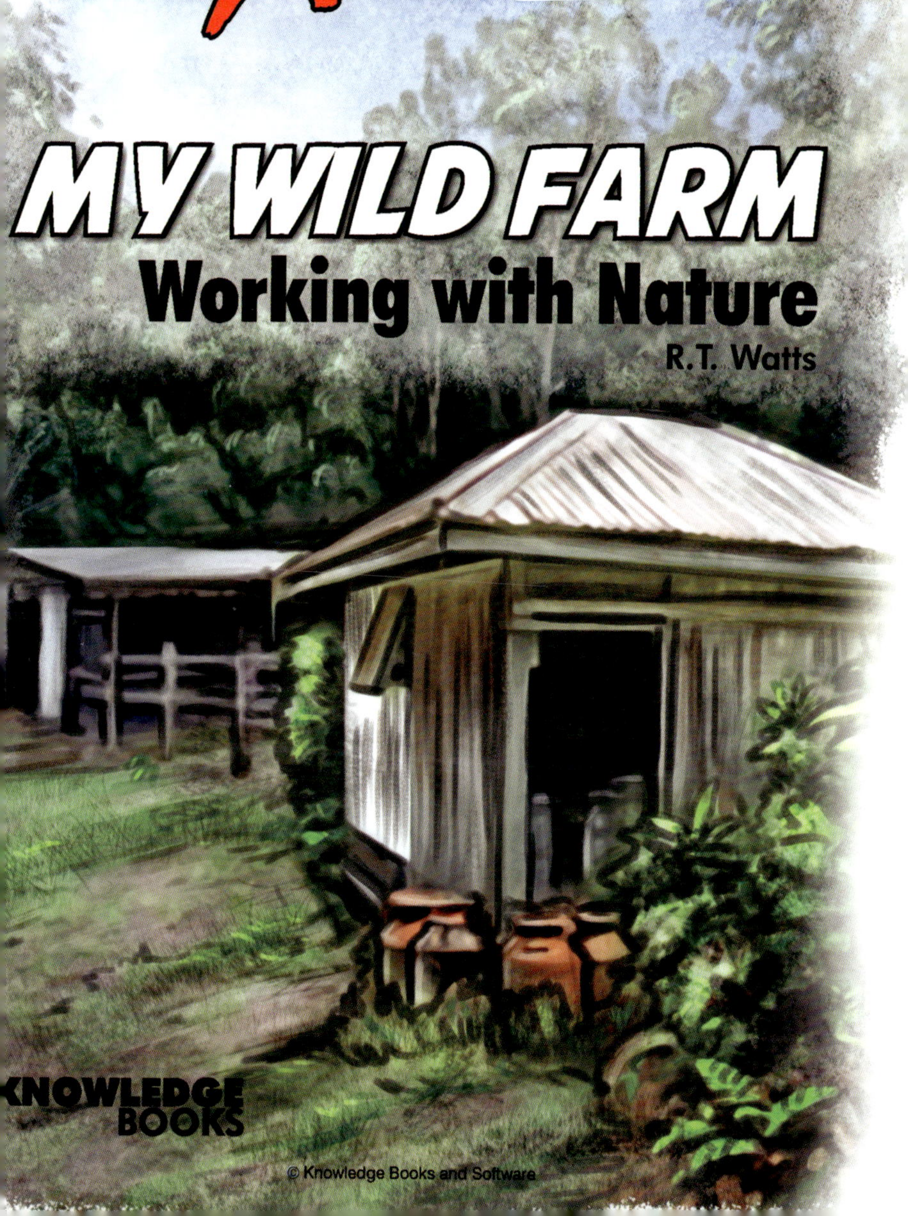

KNOWLEDGE BOOKS

Teacher Notes:

For hundreds of years, people right across the world have been clearing forests to make room for grasslands. These grasslands are used for all sorts of farming and bring food to millions of people. However, this clearing has also caused many problems for our world and people are now starting to realize how important our forests are for the health and sustainability of our planet.

Discussion points for consideration:

1. What would happen if countries across the world kept clearing forests?
2. Discuss what's happening in the Amazon Rainforest and how it's affecting the world.
3. What can you do in your community to help with rewilding in your local area?

Difficult words to be introduced and practiced before reading this book:

University, ploughing, museum, wildlife, kangaroos, wallabies, special, Antechinus, Australia, protect, curious, electric, collapsed, breakfast, quoll, amazed, possum, marsupials, nocturnal, carbon dioxide, oxygen, tropics, rainforest, population, manage, wasteland, rewilding, grazing.

Contents

1. Farm Adventures!

This story began when I was a boy. On holidays, I went to either a farm, or to the beach. My uncle and aunt had a farm that I loved to visit. I was always up early to help my uncle on his jobs. We looked after the sheep and the cattle.

I loved the big open skies and nature all around us. I loved the clean air and the great food that was cooked. I dreamed that one day I would live and work on a farm.

After I passed university, I was offered a job in a country town. It took me just three days to pack up. I was glad to leave the city.

I saw an old run-down farm for sale and bought it straight away. The old house was very sad. No one had been living there for a long time. The farm was at the end of a long road going into the mountains. It was going to be a lot of hard work!

The farm and house sat just below a big mountain. It was once a dairy farm for milking cows. Lots of old buildings had been built over the years.

Inside the barns, I found some old tools for ploughing and raking the soil. It was like being in a dusty museum. It must have been hard work for the horses and farmers.

The farm had trees growing in the fields. The forest around it was growing back. There was also lots of wildlife.

Every time I went for a walk, I would see kangaroos. They knew me but were shy and hopped away. The smaller wallabies were very fast amongst the trees.

One night I was asleep in bed. Suddenly, I felt my hair being pulled. I was so scared and rushed out of the room.

I crept back into the room to see a furry little animal trying to hide under my pillow. It was the size of a rat. It was trying to make a nest in my hair! This special, rare animal is called an Antechinus. It lives in the forests of Australia and is very shy.

2. Farm Animals Versus Wildlife!

I bought some geese to eat the grass. A giant eagle had other ideas. The eagle had a nest close to the barn. Every day it would swoop down and get its dinner.

The geese did not last very long. Any new animal on this farm was going to be eaten if I did not protect it in some way.

The old dairy seemed like the answer to protect the animals. At night, they could be safe inside. During the day, I could let them out to eat the grass.

I decided to get some pigs. The pigs loved their new house in the old dairy. They ran around in the fields eating the grass. The pigs used their snouts to dig down to get roots and worms.

Pigs are very smart animals. I found them smarter than dogs. They are curious and tricky when they want something. Some nights, they would sneak out of the dairy and crawl under the electric fence.

One night, I woke to a huge crashing sound. The whole of the back stairs had collapsed. The pigs had decided to sit on the stairs and wait for breakfast. Their weight was too much for the old stairs and they crashed down.

I needed better pens to keep my animals. All the geese were eaten by eagles. I built a hen house for some laying hens. It had been wired all around and on top.

I put all the hens and roosters in the new cage. I was happy that they were now safe. It was a lot of work, but I could now relax…but not for long!

The next night, I heard a lot of noise from the hen house. I rushed outside with my torch to check on them. I saw an animal I had never seen before. It was sitting on the roof with a dead hen.

This animal had a pointed nose with a row of sharp teeth like a chainsaw. The animal was the size of a cat. It was light brown with giant white spots. It was a rare Australian forest animal called a quoll. I was amazed to see a quoll in the wild!

In Australia, it is common to have a possum around the house. They are marsupials which means they have pouches for their babies. They are cute, furry animals with big, bushy tails.

Possums eat fruit like bananas and apples. They like to live in the ceiling of the house where it's warm and dry. They are nocturnal and sleep during the day. At night, they feed and fight and make lots of noise. This was not good for me when I had to work all day.

3. Forest Clearing

A long time ago the farm was a forest. The farmer wanted grassland and cleared the forest of all the trees. At the end of being a farm, the forest was starting to come back. Trees started growing on the grassland again.

The forest was returning to the farm. The seeds for the trees came from many different places. Some of the seeds were still in the soil. Some seeds were spread from birds eating the fruit. Other seeds were blown by the winds.

In many parts of the world, people are still clearing forests. These forests are home to wild animals and clean water. They help make the air pure.

People are still burning forests to make grasslands for beef farming. The grass is grown in the rich forest soils. The soils do not stay rich when they are grasslands. All the forest animals leave when this happens.

Forests, if left alone, are home to thousands of different plants and animals. The forest takes up carbon dioxide and gives out oxygen.

The forests of the world can take in great amounts of carbon dioxide. This helps reduce the increased amount of carbon dioxide that is in the air. Many areas of the world would be forests again if they were left to go wild.

Forests are also cleared to grow crops. In the tropics, the rainforest areas are cleared for food crops. As the population grows, more farms are needed to grow food for the people.

Many of the cleared grasslands lose their soil from water run-off. This means that more forests need to be cleared. A lot of the world's forests have now been cleared to grow food. If the land was carefully farmed, this would not happen.

The forest animals, plants, and birds help to manage the forest. They do this by spreading seeds and their waste on the soil.

When forests are removed, some of the land becomes wasteland. This is because the soil is too poor to grow crops. If the land is no longer a farm, what can it become?

4. Rewilding

Forests like those on the wild farm, can be brought back to life. How does this happen? People can help by growing trees. They can look after tree seeds and make the seeds sprout.

Forests can also be brought back to life by closing them off from farming. Fires also need to be stopped from killing the trees.

Forests will come back on old farmlands and poor grasslands. This is called rewilding. Fences must be put up to stop the grazing animals. All grazing animals will stop forests forming.

Tree seedlings need to be protected from being squashed and eaten. Fire needs to be stopped from burning and killing the little trees.

Goats can survive on poor grasslands. They are the worst animal to have near a place where you want the forest to grow. A hungry goat will eat all the leaves off a tree. They are tough animals and survive in very poor conditions. Goats do this by eating anything that they can chew.

Goats are the last animal to graze on grassland before it turns into a desert. Can a forest become a desert? Yes, and it can happen quickly. Can a desert be made back into a forest? Yes, and it can also happen quickly!

The forests of the world are our lungs. They take in the carbon dioxide and give off oxygen. The forests clean the water, so we have perfect drinking water.

Forests provide shelter and food for millions of animals and plants. My little, wild farm did not need much help to rewild. Let's rewild all those wastelands to help our Earth!

Word Bank

university
ploughing
museum
wildlife
kangaroos
wallabies
special
Antechinus
Australia
protect
curious
electric
collapsed
breakfast
quoll
amazed
possum
marsupials
nocturnal
carbon dioxide
oxygen
tropics
rainforest
population
manage
wasteland
rewilding
grazing